www.mascotbooks.com

The Artist's Alphabet

For more information, please contact:
Mascot Books
620 Herndon Parkway, Suite 320
Herndon, VA 20170
info@mascotbooks.com

Library of Congress Control Number: 2017917464

CPSIA Code: PBANG1217A
ISBN-13: 978-1-68401-714-0

Printed in the United States

Ab C D E f g H i j K L M N o p Q r s t U V W x y Z

The Artist's Alphabet

JULIA MESCHTER

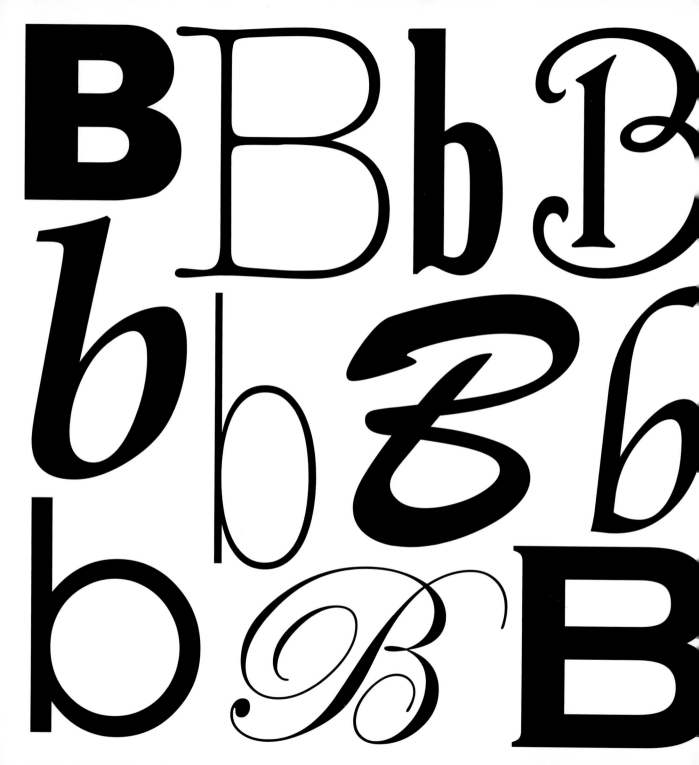

Brush

CRAYONS

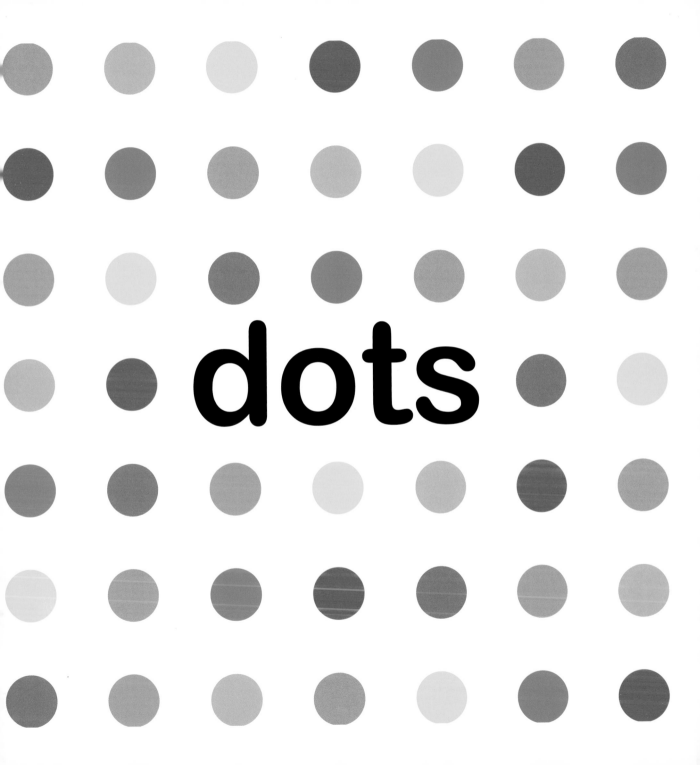

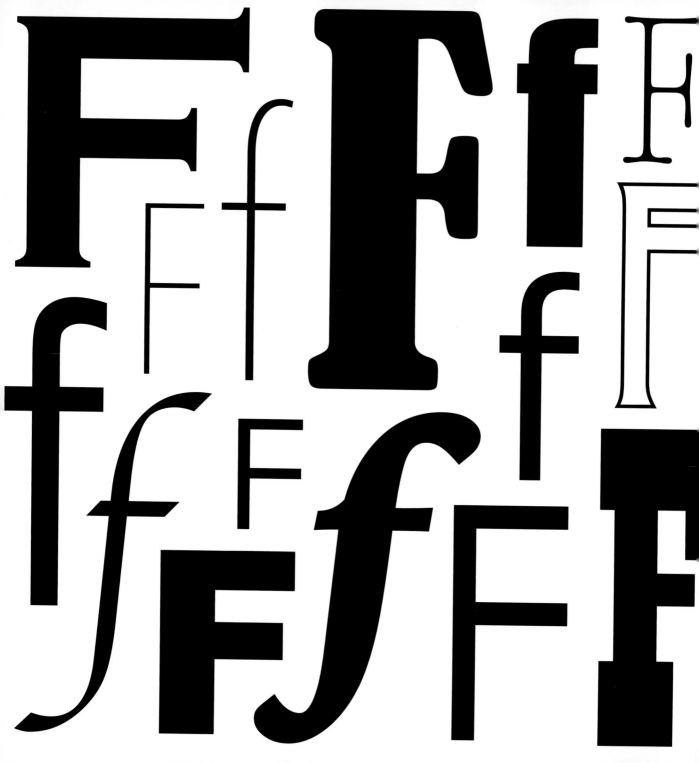

FRAME

GRAFFITI

HEXAGON

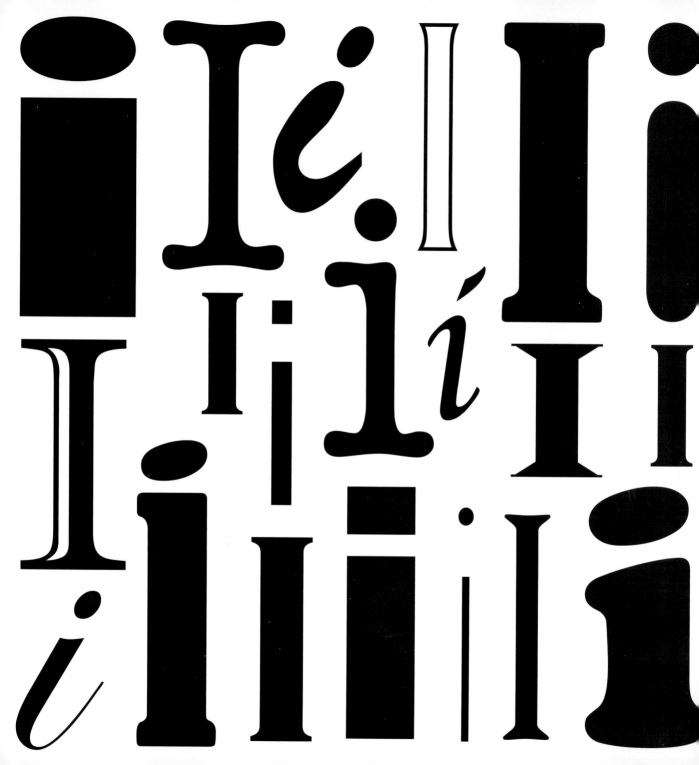

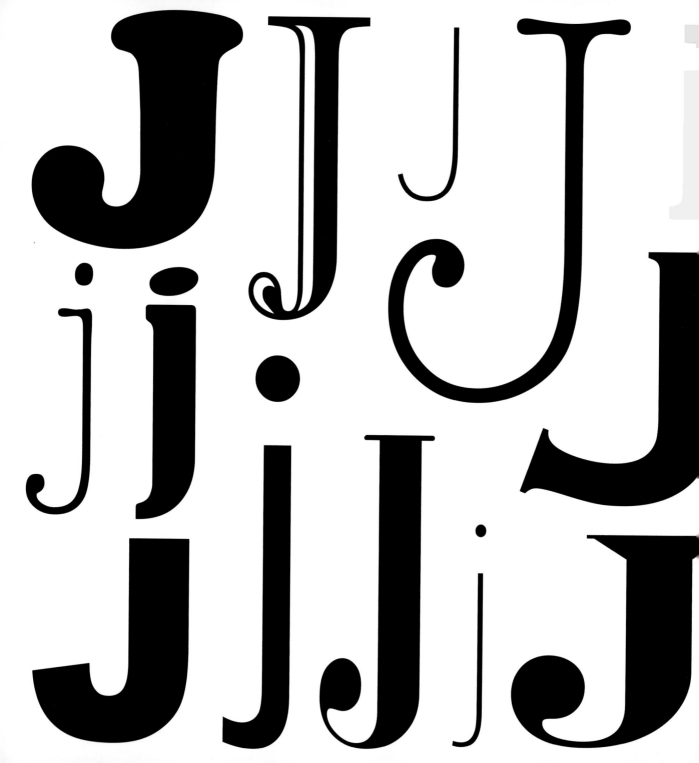

JIGSAW

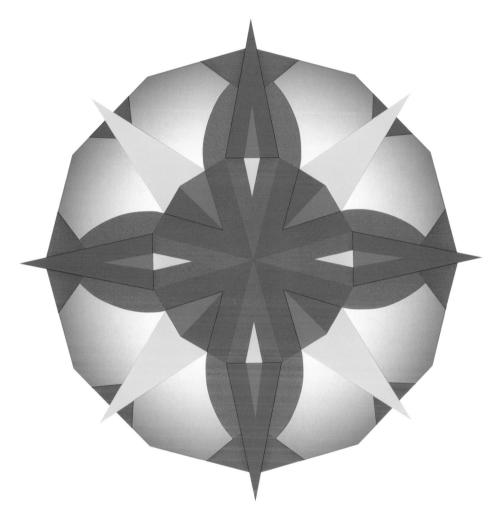

KALEIDOSCOPE

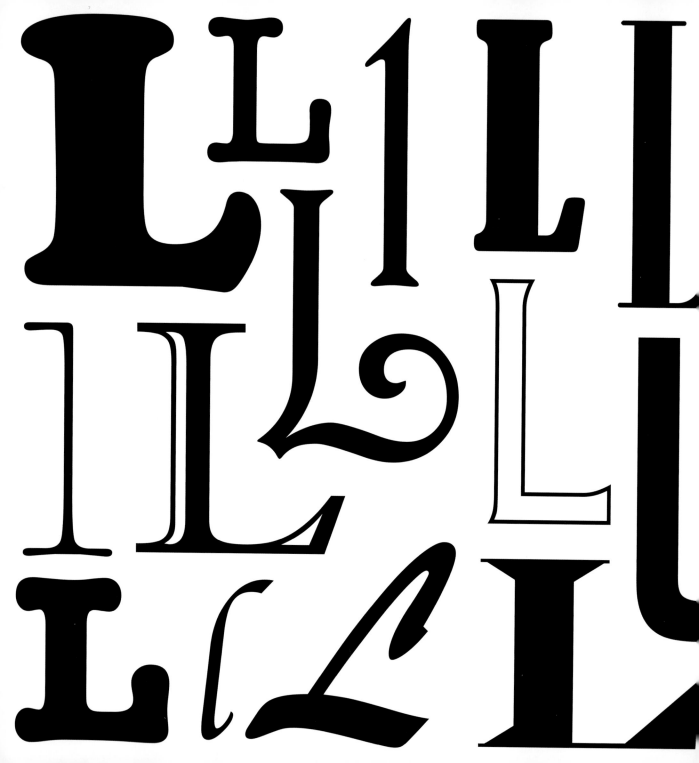

LAPTOP

MARKERS

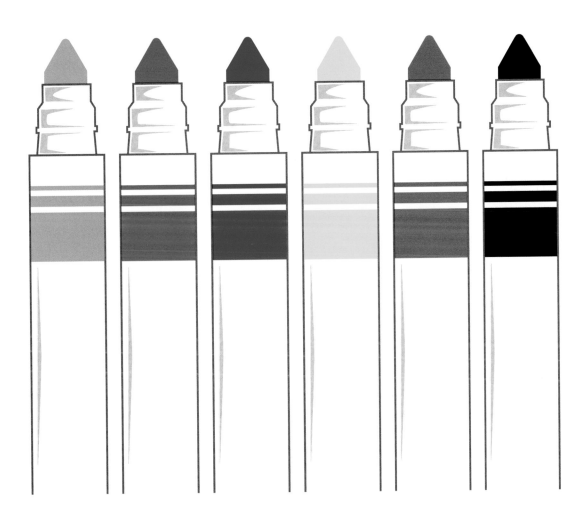

Origami

pencil

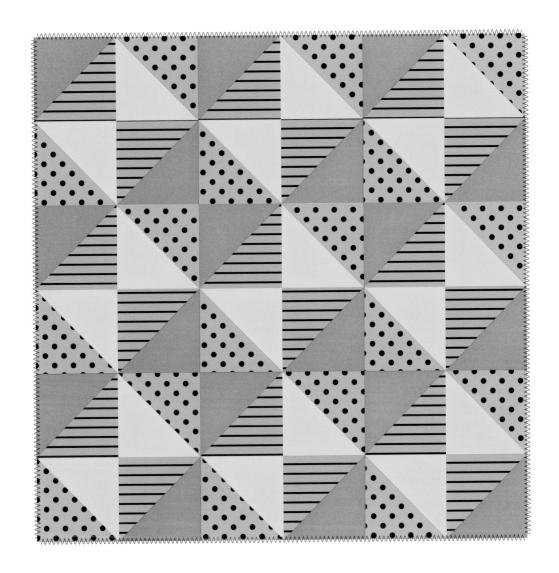

QUILT

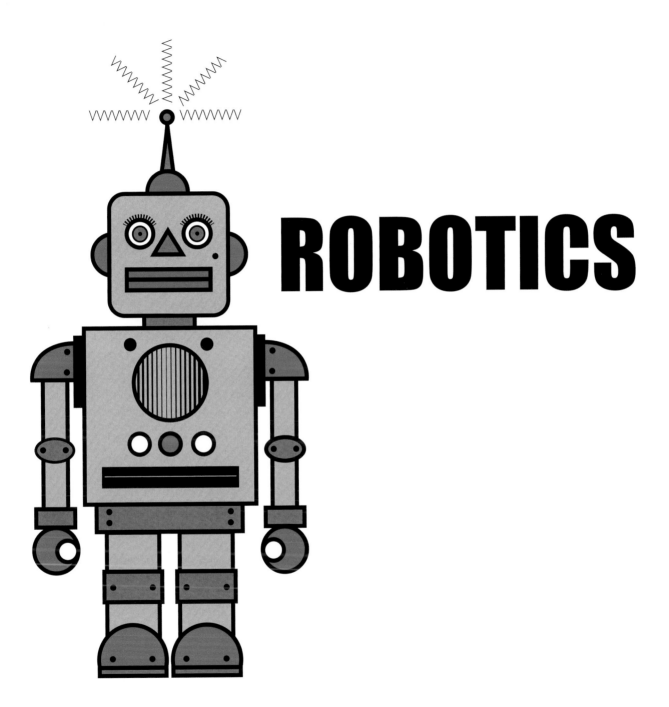

ROBOTICS

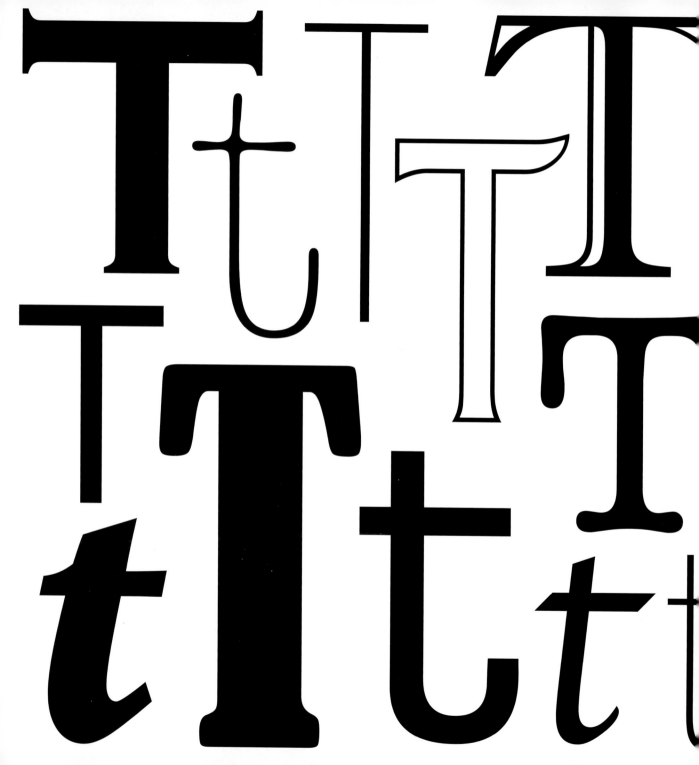

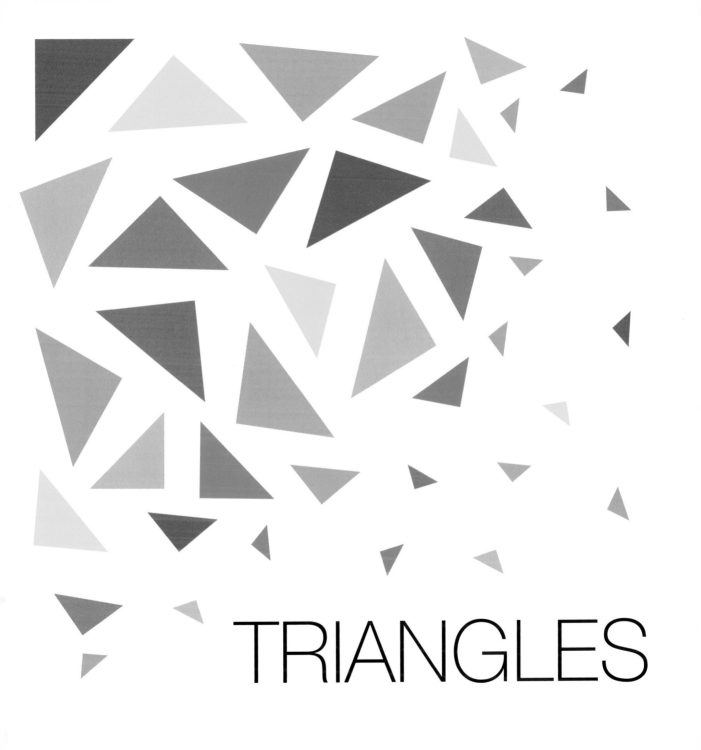

TRIANGLES

UPSIDE DOWN

UPSIDE DOWN

VIDEO GAME

WALLPAPER

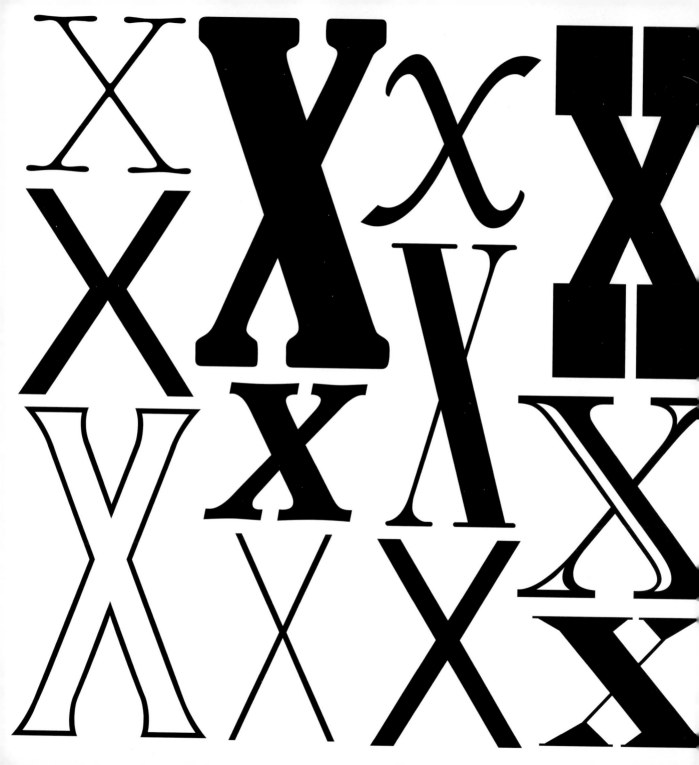

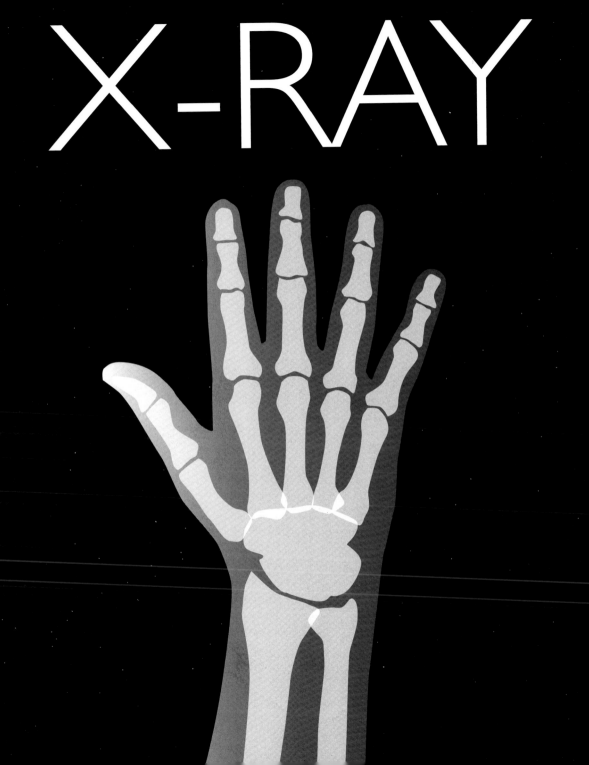

X-RAY

YELLOW

ZIGZAG

Photograph by Audrey Meschter

Julia Meschter was born in Norfolk, England.

In the last twenty years, she has lived in London, Amsterdam, and the United States as an apparel designer, most recently with NIKE, Inc.

She now lives in Portland, Oregon, with her husband and three children, who inspire her on a daily basis with their kooky, cool creativity.

This book is for them.